The Educator's Room Presents:

Keep the Fire Burning: Avoiding Teacher Burnout

Tips and Strategies From Real Teachers

Authors:

Katherine Davis

Cari Harris

Jania Hoover

Cindy Lumpkin

Lori H. Rice

Sarah J. Sorge

Franchesca Warren

ISBN: 0615778119
ISBN-13: 978-0615778112(The Educator's Room)

For more information about The Educator's Room, please visit us at www.theeducatorsroom.com.

DEDICATION

This book is dedicated to all of the teachers who feel like they can no longer make it in the classroom.
We understand.

Table of Contents

Foreword

By: Franchesca Warren

In a profession where an estimated half of all new teachers leave after the first five years, it's no wonder that teachers are suffering from teacher burn out. Every day I get emails from teachers from all across the country who leave their beloved professions citing that they can no longer 'make it' in a field that doesn't value them as a professional. Some educators leave quietly giving alternate reasons for why they quit. While others decide that they have to be the voice to all teachers scared to speak and make their reasons known for why they are leaving.

For the hundreds that leave the school system every year, there are others that choose to stay and suffer in silence. Some of them form support groups or scour the internet attempting to find articles that can help them work through their discontentment. Despite if they stay or leave, identifying a teacher suffering from burnout is easy to spot to a fellow educator. They looked haggard despite the day just starting, they constantly are searching for a new job and many times they have given up in the classroom.

According to education.com, teacher burnout is defined as a syndrome caused by the inability to cope with stressful occupational conditions -- characterized by low morale, low productivity, high absenteeism, and high job turnover. This book was written to equip teachers with specific tips and strategies to overcome this syndrome.

Take this book and not only read it but look at the lesson in every example of teachers suffering from teacher burnout. Use this book to develop a plan to not just survive your job but to find the enjoyment back in education. Recommend this book to a fellow teacher and encourage them to learn how to effectively handle burnout. Read this book during those moments when you feel like giving up and know that you have an ally in the classroom. We understand.

Chapter 1

I Was Exhausted

By: Franchesca Warren

"You can have this job! I'm done!" Those were the words of a frustrated teacher as she walked into the summer school office where I was working. I looked on in amazement as she turned in her keys, grabbed her box of personal belongings and stormed off leaving her career in education in the dust. Still a new teacher, I was in shock. I thought to myself, "What in the world made her get so frustrated that she'd quit her profession right there on the spot?" Even though watching someone walk out on their job bothered me, I just knew I'd never get to that point with teaching. I loved my career, my students and my school. What more could any teacher ask for?

However, less than five years later I was the one sitting at my desk, head in my hands seriously contemplating NEVER entering a classroom again. What had happened in just five, short years? Did I suddenly get some evil administrator that made me question my profession? Or had the kids became so unbearable that they were forcing me to leave the classroom? No, I had caught the disease that many American teachers experience, I was exhausted.

My exhaustion was affecting me in every way possible. Every morning I awoke with a nagging feeling in my stomach as I got ready for work. I went to work stressed out and left feeling even worse. I found myself so stressed out that I was spending the majority of my weekends in bed trying to get rid of migraines that seemed to come more frequently than before.

For months I had ignored these feelings and hoped that one day I'd have a 'breakthrough,' and become energized with being in the classroom again, but by Christmas, I was doubtful if that could be done. As a last resort, I decided it was time for me to take a mini vacation and try to get my ‘teaching mojo’ back. As I relaxed for those next two and a half weeks, my mind began to wonder about how I had become so exhausted in just five, short years of teaching.

I started teaching when I was just 23 years old in one of the largest, urban districts in the country. I had watched movies such as “Lean on Me”, and I just knew I could be that teacher who made a difference. So, I declined other career offers and decided to use my degree in English to teach high school English- specifically 11th grade. I was **going to be a teacher.**

I will never forget my first day of school. I left that morning excited and drove to what was going to be the longest day of my professional life. There were so many students and names that I didn't want to mispronounce. Students seemed to be shocked that I looked so young and kept asking how old I was. It seemed every moment I got more and more frazzled. For every class period I was charged with not only keeping the students who wanted to be there engaged but also the students who could care less about class. To add to my stress, it seemed like every period I got a note from the office asking me to do some task, and I had no idea what they were talking about!

To sum it up, the first day of school was hell. However, being the 'go getter' I am, I made it a mission to consume myself in teaching. I would become a Master Teacher if it killed me. So, I came to work early and left late at least four days a week. I came up to the school EVERY Saturday and held tutorial, and I was a constant fixture at games and events. I was on almost every committee at the school and helped mentor new teachers. If I missed a day, I felt guilty that my students had to go a day without me- so I came to school sick, often. I stayed up late creating quality assessments and lesson plans to make sure my students would be successful. I took the kids on field trips, and it was common for my students to call me after hours for help with their work. I was totally engulfed with my life as a teacher.

No wonder by year five, I was 'burned out' and sitting on vacation contemplating whether I even *wanted* to go back in the classroom. As I relaxed, I thought about all the careers I could have-lawyer, psychologist, etc. No matter how I saw the benefits of leaving education, I still wanted to teach children. So what would I do? Would I stay at my current school or do something that would renew my love for the classroom?

When I returned from vacation, I had a lunch meeting with my mentor and something she said 'spoke' to me. She said, "Fran, you're young. If you still want to be an educator, change cities and conquer the next chapter in your life!" All night I thought about what she said and got excited and scared. Would I really leave the only school I had ever taught at full time? What if I moved schools and hated the kids, my administration and the neighborhood? Even as I sat and thought about those variables, I knew that in order for me to overcome teacher burnout I had to make a change ASAP.

As I contemplated my move, I knew I needed to plan in order to make my plan a reality. Here are the 3 things you have to do if you want to change your surroundings to get your 'teaching mojo' back:

- **Research job opportunities.** Before uprooting your entire family, look and see what's to offer in your current area. Look for positions not only in your content area but in your district's central office. When I looked, there were few jobs for my content area, and I decided that it was too political for me to try and get a position downtown. So I knew in order for me to be happy and still be a teacher, I would probably have to move out of state.

- **Determine where you want to live.** My family and I made a list of cities where we could possibly see ourselves living. I have a family of five, so any move on my part would basically uproot their whole lives. Once we all finally decided on a city, it was time for me to find a job.

- **Research dates for job fairs.** I researched job fair dates of districts that were hiring. Looking for a new job while working a full time job is serious business, but I was determined to change my environment. For a couple of months, I constantly attended job fairs put on by school districts in the city where we were considering moving. Eventually, I received a contract. Now I could breathe.

After all my hard work, I changed cities and got the new challenge of teaching in a different environment. It was hard to tell my first school family goodbye, but changing environments allowed me to expand my professional and classroom expertise.

I didn't want to be like the teacher I had observed five years before, angrily quitting due to frustration. So I took control of my own future. In the end, I controlled my 'teaching mojo' and from now on if I wanted change, it was up to me to make it happen.

Chapter 2

Sacred Spaces, Quiet Places

By: Sarah J. Sorge

Classrooms are places of constant sound. The tap of keys on a keyboard, the muffled slide of chalk on the chalkboard, the whispered gossip of students (who believe we cannot hear them), and even the loud and boisterous group work that occasionally accompanies a science lab, or the cacophony that indicates changes in classes in a way no bell ever could.

I crave the quiet moments. I once thought myself the sort of person who could never be away from noise: a television playing in the background, music through my headphones, anything at all to make it seem like activity surrounded me. Now that I am in my fifth year of teaching, I have found that silence truly is golden… at least when I am alone. I wondered if I was becoming a sort of Grinch: "That's the one thing I hate! All the noise, noise, noise, noise!" There were days I would have given the chocolate supply in my bottom desk drawer for a few moments of quiet. I began to resent the sounds, the chatter of my students, the jarring ring of the bell, and even the whispers while I was teaching seemed deafening and grating to my shot nerves. I started getting tension headaches, and my students began to think that I did not want them anywhere near me. To some degree, maybe they were right.

I did not resent the people they were nor the stories and dramas that high school brings to them, but I did resent that I seemed to have to give my entire being to them with no respite for myself. Even my lunch breaks were somehow open to running errands for students, correcting papers, handling last-minute questions, and all the other responsibilities that teaching brings.

Keep this in mind- I love my calling as an educator, and I truly see it as something I was born to do. I love my students as if they were my own children; I wish I could tell you how many times I have felt my heart surge with pride for them or even cried with them as we lost two of our teachers to cancer. This is not something they teach you in college, that's for sure. I underestimated the emotional drain of pedagogy, and the concept of teacher burnout seemed

foreign and surreal to me. How could I burn out of the profession I love? I'm only in my late twenties, in reasonably good health, with a job that I love! That's not possible, right?
Clearly, I was wrong. The answer to my conundrum was simple: sensory overload.

I have studied neuroscience in the laboratory, and my academic passion is educational neurobiology. I could not believe that I had overlooked the very thing I studied: my brain. The center of my emotional core, the nucleus of my teaching abilities was being ignored in favor of being everything to everyone who crossed my path. I became a surrogate parent to my students and, like a parent, I grew tired. I had placed all my focus on picking them up, dusting them off, cheering them on, scolding them, occasionally feeding them, and smiling every step of the way. While doing this, I inadvertently neglected myself. I thought: *the students need me far more; I can use my free period of the day and do this for them*. Or, *I should go to work because they need me far more than my bed does; I'll get better while I work, and they won't have to deal with a substitute teacher*. These are the simple sacrifices that every teacher makes, and it's often these sacrifices that can have the most profound impact. Some of our students may see this, but most don't, and the whole time we give beyond ourselves for their benefit. Admittedly, it often seems that we work a thankless job where we are criticized and taken for granted.

The administration places demands on us, too. We are asked to volunteer at charity events, plan field trips, chaperone the Prom, and smile at parents at open house. We need to be ready to field parent concerns via phone calls, emails, and drop-in visits. Our state standards are updated more than the coffee in our coffee pots, and just when we think we have it all under control, we have to head up a fundraiser so we can buy supplies. Among these demands we have papers to correct, labs to set up, and the latest requests from the main office that are dumped in our laps at the very last-minute. This doesn't even include the increasing concern over teacher evaluations that are heavily based on high-stakes testing as benchmarks for student success, instead of overall classroom progress. There are times I've held my head in my hands at my desk, a stack of papers in front of me to correct and thought, "This isn't the job I thought it was going to be. There aren't enough hours in the day and too little of me to go around."

Is it any surprise, then, that most new teachers are ready to quit in their first 5 to 7 years of the profession? Are the veteran teachers who stuck it out and stayed in the teaching game a little tattered around the emotional edges? Are teachers in general closer to bitter rather than simply tired? There's evidence of it each time we enter the schools. Our teacher lounges have become locations for group therapy amidst rushed lunches; we shiver with dread when we hear our names called to the front office to meet with the principal or vice-principal; we find our eyes shifting to the clocks to pray for the day to pass just a little faster. I've found myself, occasionally, responding to the jovial "How goes today?" with "Eh, I'm hanging in there." I didn't mention that I was hanging by my fingernails, praying for a reprieve, hoping that the final bell of the day was a whisper away rather than hours ahead of me. I saw my lack of teaching verve and creativity to be a failure of mine rather than a product of my environment. This self-debasing thinking only proved to drive me further into the burnout, and I was having difficulty finding a way out of it.

It turns out this negativity wasn't my fault; I was a victim to a stressful environment. As teachers, we are constantly subject to sensory overload. We know about our senses: sight, taste, touch, sound, and smell. Think about each of those senses and how they are assaulted on a daily basis in our schools. Usually, we are able to handle all of this: the bickering couple in the hallway, the crying child who doesn't want to leave her parents, the football player yelling to his buddy at the other end of the hallway, the bells, the loudspeakers with announcements, computer screens, backpacks thudding to the floor, chemical smells from the Biology and Chemistry rooms even the lunch cooking in the cafeteria. It all makes me want to shout, "All the noise, noise, noise, noise, noise!"

It occurred to me rather recently that I was starting to suffer a bit of burnout because I was not listening to my brain. The tension headaches I felt, my irritability, my racing heart... all of these symptoms were the ways my brain was saying, "I can't keep up anymore! Time out!" I realized that in order to be an effective educator, my students deserved a teacher whose nerves weren't so fried that I could practically smell the crisped edges.

Here are some ways I dealt with the sensory overload:

- **Make your classroom as much about you as it is about your students.** One of the ideas in brain-based education research is that a classroom should be an inviting environment for students where they do not feel threatened; instead, they should feel safe and invited. It should be the same for teachers. Because we're such a self-sacrificing lot of individuals, we tend to set ourselves on the wayside, even in our own rooms. As a result, we create classroom environments that are inviting for our students, but not for ourselves. I decided that I needed to make a place in my room that was inviting for me as the teacher. What better place, then, was my desk? I started creating a "sacred space" there. "This area," I said to myself, "is mine."

- **Establish some personal space.** Simple changes do not have to be elaborate or expensive. You do not have to break the bank in order to create a space to call your own. First, I made it clear to my students that while they could come up to my desk to ask questions or speak to me privately, anything on it or in the near vicinity of it was off-limits. They were not to place anything on my desk; hand it to me instead. No, you may not just take a pen off my desk; ask me first.

  Little things like that helped denote boundaries for my students. If you create a sacred space for yourself, it has to be a place where you don't worry about things being moved or taken without consent. Once I had established a boundary, I began to make my desk area something that would be soothing for me and remind me of good things I've done.

- **Personalize your space.** If you look at my desk area, you'll see a hanging crystal chakra sun-catcher that is suspended from the pendulum string attached to my ceiling. One of my students found out that I collect unicorns, so she drew me a unicorn to put on my desk. I taped it down nearby to my coffee mug. Next to that lovely drawing, I placed a poem that always inspired me. I also have a constant urge to be near water, so I placed a water fountain in my desk area, too. The flow of water reminds me to be adaptable, and the sound of it is very soothing. I placed an ivy plant on my windowsill recently in order to draw nature indoors. A green plant can bring life to a room that is rarely much more than cinderblock walls and student desks.

- **Treat your senses!** In my sacred space, I have addressed sight (the crystals, drawing, and poem) and sound (the flow of water in my desktop fountain). To help ease my taste overload, occasionally I'll reward myself with a piece of my favorite chocolate from a desk drawer. It reminds me that rewards are acceptable, especially ones you give yourself. There is nothing wrong with treating yourself; you do not have to give everything up for your students. I also have a coffee pot in my storage area so that I can have a hot cup exactly how I like it. To some people this may seem minor, but to me it meant a lot.

Getting the smell right was tricky. Coffee brewing is great, but I can't have it running all day. Instead, I invested in a timer air freshener and placed my favorite scent inside-apple. My students love it, saying that I have one of the nicest smelling classrooms in the whole school. By making my classroom smell like someplace I want to go, as soon as I open the door in the morning I'm greeted with a comforting scent. Last but not least was touch. In my classroom you will find objects like brain-teasers, plush animals (an otter and couple penguins), or even just a ball so that I can focus my energy into touching a soothing object. Even though you can't touch it, I have a basketball-sized puffer fish hanging from the ceiling. It makes me smile, and that is enough reason to keep it hanging.

For the most part, my students abide well by the "please don't touch my space" request I made, and you can do the same by setting boundaries. Find a couple of objects that make you calm and happy; keep them nearby. When you feel yourself getting stressed out, focus your nervous energy on that object and think of something more positive. Take a breath and take a small mental vacation: go to the beach in your mind, imagine a meal you had recently that tasted divine, or anticipate meeting friends later for very bad karaoke… anything that can bring you into a more positive state is worth that energy focus.

- **Take time for yourself**. Lastly, do not underestimate the restorative power of shutting and locking your classroom door, turning off the lights, and just using your free period or lunch as a time to enjoy silence. I know this is not always possible, but your brain will thank you if you do this, and you'll find yourself more restored than when you began. Ultimately, this will make you a more effective teacher because you managed to ease all of the sensory overload, and your brain was given time to process information at its own pace and under its own terms. I've learned that doing such things is a great way to relieve tension headaches. Remember this: you are not antisocial if you decide to spend lunch away from the faculty room. Your colleagues will not think less of you; they've been in your position, too, so you're not alone in the need for quiet.

Do not be afraid to do something for yourself inside your classroom to help make the daily stressors you face to be far more tolerable. Create your own sacred, quiet place where you are able to retreat and let the sensory issues slide away like water over smooth stones. You might even catch yourself saying, "*Ah, no more noise,noise,noise, noise!*"

Chapter 3

What Do I Make? A Difference!

By: Lori H. Rice

Teaching has always been my passion. I worked a few odd jobs in college to pay the bills, but I have generally always taught. In my youth, I was involved in Bible School and babysitting. I was a camp counselor. Planning activities, reading, playing, questioning, watching children think and learn are my favorite things to do. There is a deep rooted inner part of me that IS a teacher. Without teaching, I am not sure what I would be. So why then, do I question this profession? Why do I feel so fed up with it, and why do I think about what else I can do? Why do I often wonder what other jobs are out there? What is happening in the educational system that good teachers are leaving?

I have been teaching for sixteen years. Every system has amazing and not so amazing components. Every profession has positives and negatives. Working in the public eye, however, teachers are open to an unbelievable amount of criticism. We were all once students, we have all been in a classroom, so isn't everyone an expert on education? That mentality has driven common respect for teachers into the ground. The lack of respect contributes to the media opinion, unsupportive parents, and overall negative views of teachers. It is this negative factor forcing many teachers to leave the profession. When my personal image is one of a selfless, giving, caring teacher, but society's overall image is negative, I question why I give so much. I know I am not alone in this struggle.

So let's first look at the ever important dollar. A friend of mine once said, "You can turn anything into a lesson." When I am on vacation or summer break, I constantly think about what I can bring to my students. At conferences, I ask for extra pencils or rulers or company freebies for the prize box. During holidays, I research to learn more about a subject, or look for lessons, or read a chapter book to discuss with a reading group. I think of ways to repurpose materials to turn them into educational games and activities. Throw something away? No thank you! We can use that in our classroom to learn! I spend my own time and money on my kids… yes, they are MY kids. But if you listen to the media, you may get the opinion that

I am a gold digger. You may think that any classroom money is used to purchase velvet couches and large screen TV sets for the teacher "lounge." Society's perception of the money spent in schools is not reality. This ever draining negative image of the American teacher filters into my perception of what I do, and causes me to wonder what other jobs are out there.

Next, let's look at scores. My students amaze me with their knowledge and creativity. I believe in working in groups and creating projects. I think asking a good question can tell you more about what a student knows than a perfect score on a multiple choice test. I know students learn when they are excited and interested, and those qualities along with creativity and respect are fostered in my classroom. However, matching that with requirements and regulations is the challenge. I know applying the skills and evaluating the content will hold that knowledge in their hearts. It is important to respect your own teaching philosophy and match that with the standards and demands of the test. It is possible to teach with creativity and passion and higher level thinking skills and tie in your standards. This gap between what is expected and what we know is best teaching practice is exhausting though.

Soon, this stress began to impact how I was teaching and something had to be done in order for me to continue. I reached a point where I had three choices: succumb to the negative energy and go down with the ship, find a new job and abandon my profession, or focus my energy and lead the way. I am not a negative person, and I am not a quitter, so choice three was my option. I decided to become an active part in making changes in my educational world.

Taking small steps to make changes under your control can make an enormous difference. Here are a few changes I made:

- **Combat the negativity from society and the media by making a decision to find positive influences.** This is possible if you make decisions to surround yourself with positive people and stay away from negative people. I made a change in grade level and buildings to change the administrative influences I was working under. I found positive quotes and posted those on Facebook. This in turn brought positive comments from friends and colleagues. I focused on the positive things in my classroom and the growth my students were making. I made a conscious effort to avoid negative talk and to turn to positive or leave a conversation when it became negative. An opinion can only have an impact on you if you let it and I decided to learn from the negative by focusing on the positive.

- **Find resources that can encourage you**. A few years later, I had the great fortune to be invited to become part of a group of teachers doing a book study on Courage to Teach, by Parker Palmer. The focus of this book is about listening to your inner teacher. I read the book and joined the conversation. There are many wonderful publications for educators with positive messages. Find one that grabs your interest, treat yourself to a cup of your favorite beverage and take the time to read. Reading Courage to Teach and reflecting on myself as a teacher was an empowering experience. This book reaffirmed that I was on the right path to make changes around me.

- **Make the decision to say yes!** I thought about my personal teaching philosophy and reexamined why I became a teacher. I believe in questioning and thinking and learning. I believe in hands-on experiences and students centered activities. I decided to make commitments to become involved in committees and activities that support this philosophy. I reexamined the efforts I was a part of in my district, and if they did not align or support this philosophy, then I requested to be removed or I did not participate in that discussion. You don't have control over everything; there are committees and teams you are put on without your choice.

  Instead, I became proactive in volunteering for groups that matched my philosophy, and that helped balance out the situations that did not align as closely to my professional philosophy. As I opened conversation to make changes from committees and groups I no longer wanted to be as active with, I had more time to focus on those I did. Look over your list of responsibilities, committees, groups, after school activities. Commit to those that support your philosophy and find ways to become less involved (or better yet remove yourself entirely) from those that do not. Saying yes when my philosophy matches the goals has reaffirmed my inner teacher.

I graduated third in my HS class and held a 4.0 my first year of college. I excelled in math and science classes. Engineering, medicine, even being a lawyer (my siblings would tell you I excel at arguing my point) were all well within my reach and possibilities for a future career. **BUT I CHOSE TEACHING.** I made a very well thought out, conscious decision to become an educator. Maybe for you as well, it was also a calling, a decision, and the right choice. Learning is exciting to me. I am an example of lifelong learning for my kids. This is the person I know should be reflected to society. It does not always match the vision of media.

However, the opinion of society is that one becomes a teacher when there is not another option. According to Taylor Mali's first person account on You Tube, there is a story of a group of friends and acquaintances sitting around after dinner talking. The overall opinion of the speaker is those who *can*, do, and those who *can't,* teach. Another guest at the table, a teacher, is asked, "What do you make?" The response is a list of items that are not measurable. Teachers make inspiration, creativity, wonder, writers, readers, philanthropists, productive members of society. These are the things we have the honor of seeing, participating in, doing, and being a part of in our classrooms.

Teachers make futures. There is not another profession that can declare that. We touch every single student in our classrooms as well as families beyond our walls. For many of you, these are the very reasons you get up every morning and walk through doors that sometimes seem too heavy to open. Why do I teach? Because it is the only profession on this planet where I get to touch the future each and every day, see the frustration and rewarding joy of a new skill learned, and watch individuals bloom into that which they are meant to be. What do I make? The answer is simple; I make a difference!

Chapter 4

My Job Matters

By: Katherine Davis

Teaching is a very noble profession, and I am honored to be a part of it. I am honored to be in a position where I can make a difference. There is no better feeling than when I witness my students applying something they have learned in my class, or listening to them tell me that what I taught them helped them in some way. This is what it's all about. This is what others should recognize about teaching. But, this is not always the case. There are some people who do not hold the teaching profession in such high regard and voice their opinions at every opportunity they get. This is not only frustrating, but it has often times made me question why I am still teaching.

There have been a few occasions where someone will offer their not-so-nice opinion of my profession. Is it too much to want people to find teaching as meaningful as it really is?

I recently found myself in the company of someone who did not think that teaching was a good idea. "So, what do you do?" asked a somewhat friendly person (who I'll refer to as Carol). I replied enthusiastically and with a huge grin because I'm proud, "I teach!" Carol stared blankly at me, blinking about every 3 seconds while softly killing my pride and said, in a tone that makes me look like I'm the most pathetic person in the place, "Ohhhh! Why would you ever want to teach? What made you get into that? How do you tolerate those kids?"

I started to respond, "Well…I …"

But Carol interrupted, "What you need to do is find something to do that really matters."

My initial thought was, "I know this_____ (insert very colorful language here)." But instead I calmly said, "So, you're one of those." However, the look on Carol's face was full of shock, disbelief, and a little repulsiveness when I returned the favor by asking, "Well, what is it that you do?" I then quickly followed the question with the same remarks she had so graciously offered me.

Everything in me wanted Carol to experience what being a "professional outcast" felt like. Once the initial stage of shock wore off, Carol apologized while I laughed at the lesson I'd spontaneously taught her. And to think that this person thought that teaching didn't matter.

People who have never spent a day in education are the quickest to tell me what I should be doing, and/or how I should do my job. They feel as though their opinion on my profession is the end-all, be-all and should dictate my work. Does this only happen to Educators? I wonder how many other professions get told how to do their jobs by people who have never worked in their field?

Far too often, I find myself defending my beloved profession. It is as if I have to convince people that I have a "real job" and that my job makes a difference. I have to assure them that my job is important and that my job deserves a little recognition. I find myself getting angry and bothered by the lack of respect the teaching profession encounters. I get offended because some people take my passion for a joke and choose to highlight every negative aspect they "hear" about it. I want to look these people in the eye and shout for every teacher, "*You're welcome!*"... in hopes that the light bulb will go off. I wonder if walking around bundled in a cardboard sign while randomly yelling, "*Teachers rock!*" will get my point across. If it were not for the teaching profession, could any other profession exist?

Yes, the frustration that comes with not being treated as a professional drives me absolutely crazy, and sometimes I want to throw my hands up and release myself from this madness. But if I quit, what happens to my students?

I teach because teaching is what I am supposed to do. It's a commitment that I have chosen to be a part of. For eight years of my life, I have been committed to education. I've never cheated, although the thought has occurred to me on many occasions, I'm still here.

It takes a strong, dedicated, passionate person to do what a teacher does. The constant overtime, the early mornings and late nights, the sacrifices, the children and their problems…this job is not for the weak. When everything that makes up this profession comes crashing down on you, remember why you teach. Your job matters to those who get the most out of it…your students.

Am I crazy?

No.

I am a teacher, and my job also matters.

When others disregard what it takes to be a teacher, finding the time to find meaning in your job can definitely add to teacher burnout. With all of the other frustrations that come with this profession, having a reason to stay can get lost. If your job loses meaning, how do you find it again?

- **Remember what you do in your classroom.** My first year of teaching was exactly what I expected. I was a ball full of nerves; I constantly doubted myself, and I had absolutely no idea what I was supposed to do with the group of 7th graders that were now my responsibility. However, my 7th graders made me feel like the best thing since ice cream. They were so full of life and inspiration that it was easy to walk into that classroom and teach. There was no judgment in that room, no negativity, just learning. The indescribable feeling of pure joy and accomplishment that comes when the light bulb goes on for your students, and you see that they are learning is priceless.

- **Do not take everything people say about education to heart.** As teachers, we are extra sensitive when it comes to the world of education. Over the years, I have had to learn that everyone does not have the same feelings for education that I have. They do not understand where I am coming from when I say "I absolutely love what I do" and that "I do not see myself doing something that does not involve education." It really bothered me how people disregarded the importance of education. A seasoned educator once said to me, "It is so wonderful to see such passion in you young, fresh teachers, but it is equally devastating to see this same passion wasted on unnecessary explanation. Keep that passion for things that matter because it's no good elsewhere."

- **Take the time to find the meaning you have lost.** Reevaluating yourself and your purpose for teaching is okay. There is a reason why you became a teacher, and it does not hurt to revisit that reason from time-to-time. Make time to regroup. If this means taking a day off, DO IT! It is a lot easier to regroup when you are not in the mist of the madness. Besides, you are way more effective when you have had some time to put things back into perspective.

Chapter 5

Let's Get Together (Yah, Yah, Yah)!

By: Cari Harris

After an English test with particularly disastrous results, the teacher scolds the class and then she asks that everybody who thinks that they are not particularly good at English to stand up. For quite a while, all the students just look at each other, but nobody moves. Finally, little Johnny slowly stands up. "Very good, Johnny", says the teacher, "at least you realize where your weakness is and that gives you an opportunity to improve." "Oh, but I don't think I'm very bad at English, Madam," says Johnny, "but I simply felt sorry for you standing there all alone."

Most teachers would never find themselves in a position of pointing out students' weaknesses publicly – such methods long ago went out of style. However, teachers 'standing there all alone' are still all too common. We start off so excited to be teaching, and we cheerily begin our careers with the noble ideals of skilled educators ready to take on the world. Over time, endless faculty meetings, required professional development in-services, and curriculum mandate upon curriculum mandate temper our excitement. Many of us find ourselves buried under weeks of test preparation instead of poetry writing, standardized quizzing instead of role-playing a UN assembly, and hours of multiple choice practice instead of using geometry to design a house. Soon, all we want to do is close that classroom door and just *be* with our students. Or sometimes, we simply want to block out everything so we can just get something *done*.

A tremendous isolation can build up over years of closing the classroom door and cutting ourselves off from the hallway outside. Burnout seeps into the crevices of our teaching career so easily when we fall into the trap of purely solo work. Often, we also begin to feel proprietary about what we create: our curriculum, our lesson plans, and our assessments. After a while, we don't open the door as easily for colleagues, we grudgingly go to department meetings or professional development, and we get tired, run down and stressed. One of the easiest ways to avoid burnout like this is to avoid the isolation in the first place.

I had been teaching only three or four years when I noticed myself becoming more and more isolated in my classroom. I never went to the faculty lounge, I spent lunch at my desk (often with students in the room), I came in early and left late, all in an effort to just be the kind of teacher I wanted to be. It was easy to become cynical about Professional Learning Teams or department meetings when all too often, the results seemed disconnected from what was really happening in the classroom. I really wasn't connecting with my colleagues in any productive way, and though I *thought* I was doing well, I felt more and more alone.

I finally realized that making an effort to engage with my colleagues would open the door and allow me to learn more and be more confident about my teaching. I began to initiate opportunities to collaborate. I asked for ideas, even if I already had my own – it couldn't hurt to see what was going on in other rooms. I looked for ways to share what was happening in my classroom in the hopes my colleagues would do the same. I made sure to eat lunch at least once a week with one of my fellow teachers, rather than stay holed up in my room. Slowly, I didn't feel so alone anymore.

Collaboration is the key to curing the curse of isolated burnout. But this is often easier said than done. Our culture encourages the independent, self-sufficient worker. Movies and "reality" television praise those who get to the top all on their own, even if they have to step on others to get there. The business world lauds the self-made man, and protects his proprietary knowledge and creations. But there is another, rising collaborative idea that has gained traction in recent decades: open sourcing. Made famous in the computing world by Linus Torvalds, the operating system Linux is a prime example of the success of open sourcing. In 1991, he released his base code of the Linux-based operating system to the world and invited everyone to join in improving and perfecting it. Twenty years later, more than 90% of the world's 500 fastest supercomputers run on some version of Linux, and most servers and mainframes also run it. The idea of open sourcing is that the more that experts in a field work together on an idea, the better its culminating product will be.

Teaching can work the same way, and when it does, burnout has a far smaller chance of success. Successful collaboration requires teachers willing to share not only ideas, but also actual materials, planning, and practices. It creates a space where the cooperative teachers cannot only learn from each other but help each other bear the weight of the multitude of requirements put upon them. It can lead to more effective teaching, assessing and data collection. All of this adds up to creating more expertise in the field, and less chance of isolation burnout. Here are some ways to approach collaboration if you're new to it:

- **Start with respect for your colleagues and their work**. You may have had little chance to see your fellow teachers in action, or view their lesson plans or materials. You may only know them from conversations in the faculty room, or department meetings. Start with a fresh slate – and make your foundation an initial respect for their efforts to be effective teachers just like you. Remember, they are just as tired, stressed, and isolated as you often feel. But they can make valuable contributions and help you to think about things in a new way. Just a change in point-of-view can refresh your teaching spirit.

- **Reach out and engage your colleagues in collaboration**. Look for opportunities to work together and find ways to listen to what other teachers have to say. Even teachers in different subject areas can offer new perspectives on your own ideas. Request to see what they've done, and try out some of their ideas. A professional community needs to have dynamic back and forth, and you can create that by being willing to hear your colleagues out, and establish a trust relationship with them.
- **Be positive and authentic**. Teachers don't have time for BS, and we all know how awful teaching conditions can be sometimes. Collaboration should be a time for focusing on what's possible, not what is weighing you down. But be real about it. Share real experiences of how your ideas have worked or not worked. If you try something together, don't embellish the results; give authentic reports to each other so that you can work to continuously perfect your practice. Positive feedback is always a mechanism for more collaboration in the future.

- **Ask "Why?" and "What?"** Make your collaboration time inquiry-based. Ask lots of "why are we doing this?" questions to each other. Meaningful ideas come out of meaningful questions, and with so little time for creativity in the classroom these days, it's all the more important to help each other with thoughtful ideas. The result is also a key focus for a successful collaboration. "What?" is the question about your end product. What can you create and share together that will ease your workloads and help you become more effective? The idea is to support each other into better teaching practices.

Sharing may not come easily for you. That's okay. However, try it anyway. Share a lesson plan with a new teacher. Ask someone down the hall what they do in a certain situation with a student. Reach out and create space for collaboration. Teachers who share the burdens of educating young people are teachers who don't feel so isolated at the end of the day. Don't suddenly find yourself standing alone in your classroom with the door closed. Seek out your colleagues and open the door to a fresh perspective, new ideas and shared experiences. Burnout won't even have a chance.

Chapter 6

Switching Things Up: An Individualized Transition Plan (ITP)

By: Cindy Lumpkin

As I set with my eyes closed at my desk, enjoying the last five minutes of my lunch period, I recalled what would ultimately be the best advice I ever received from my college professor. I could see with great detail old Mr. Johnson with his coke bottle glasses looking out at us as he sat on his desk lecturing. It was always difficult to tell when he was actually looking at you. His big eyes, magnified by his bifocals, were cockeyed. I always felt embarrassed when he would motion by pointing or nodding his head in my direction to respond in class. Not being sure his gesture was for me, I would look behind or to the side of me before responding. The funny thing is there were only four of us in class, so no one was ever behind me.

I found Mr. Johnson to be extremely boring and often daydreamed in his class. He was unreasonable with assignments and his overall expectation of us. But that day was different. It was the day he briefly discussed teacher burnout in the field of special education. He was the only professor that I recall who even remotely spoke on the subject. To be honest, I am not sure what made this short lecture different or out of the two years I had him for at least four classes why I remember this day and his words: "Teaching students with disabilities is hard work. The paperwork is grueling. Most teachers don't last five years in the classroom. I would recommend you switch things up every four to five years or else you will find yourself exhausted and teaching will no longer be a joy."

After almost ten years into my career as a special education teacher and after the recent birth of my precious baby, his words couldn't have been truer. I dreaded coming to work! I hated my Advisor (fancy word for Homeroom); I detested Tuesday faculty meetings, and by this time, refused to have anything to do with any extracurricular activity. Not even the threats from my principal that all teachers had to attend PTA meetings were enough for me to do anything beyond my 8:15 a.m. to 3:45 p.m. day. I was exhausted!

"How did I get to this point?" I asked myself. I had done what Mr. Johnson advised. Not on purpose, but nevertheless, I "switched things up." I started my career teaching a self-contained class of MOID (Moderately Intellectually Disabled) students. I enjoyed those students. They were fun, and we did lots of community trips. But an unwanted transfer changed that only a few months into the year. However, my next assignment was Heaven sent. I started working with students with mild disabilities (Mildly Intellectually Disabled, Specific Learning Disabilities, ADHD, etc.). Although they were still self-contained, I only taught two subjects. They rotated classes like everyone else.

I had the opportunity to flex my "expert" teacher muscles a little by identifying a student who was mislabeled. Although I had limited teaching experience, old Mr. Johnson had done his job well. Where I was lacking in practical experience, I more than made up for with textbook knowledge. It only took me to evaluating a few assignments by C.W. to know that I wasn't dealing with a student with an intellectual disability, but a textbook dyslexic. The process of getting this student labeled correctly should have given me a glimpse into the bureaucracy of a major urban school system. Yet still, I will never forget the pride in seeing C.W. correctly labeled, and eventually, the successful transition into the general education setting. I even convinced him to try out for the JV basketball team. He had always wanted to play, and he had the build; he was tall. Like many students, having the label of "special" took every ounce of confidence the poor fellow had. With a philosophy that academics without confidence wouldn't get too many people far, I incorporated ways to build my students confidence. C.W. responded well. He tried out and made the JV squad as a sophomore in high school; he blossomed like a flower in spring time.

There were other successes too. Unintentionally, I found out how to win parents over just by seeing the best in their students, despite the negatives. All first communications with a parent have to be positive. Each year, I personally called all the parents of the students on my caseload as well as the parent those who were in the classes I taught.

> "Hello, this is Mrs. Lumpkin from Somewhere High School. May I speak to the parent or guardian of Someone Destined?
>
> "Hi, I just wanted to call and introduce myself to you. I am so excited about teaching Someone Destined this school year. I've been looking over his file and see all the skills he learned last year as well as the many strengths he possesses. I know he will make great strides this year as well. Hey! I know you're busy, but when you get time I would love to meet you as well."

Believe it or not, that one five minute conversation started a solid foundation that I was able to build on throughout the year with many of my students' parents. Now, not every conversation I had with parents of my student was as positive, but I made so many positive deposits before the negative calls started that their ears where always open to hear me. I could have made up untruths about their children, and they would have believed me. One of my students' parents even told me, "Mrs. Lumpkin you have my permission to beat him." That made me laugh, and I explained that I couldn't do that, but she insisted. Well, I did the only thing I could do. I told the student what his mother said. He laughed too, he knew I couldn't nor would I have, but whenever I had to get him back in line, reminding him of what power his mother had entrusted me with sure helped.

"Switching things up," I did. After two years of teaching, my then principal asked me to chair the Student Support Team (SST), and I was also coaching the school's Volleyball team. As chair of SST, my teacher workload was cut in half so that I could fulfill my duties in this new position. I was now working with both students with disabilities and their general education peers. I loved the diversity, and the new duties where refreshing. It made me a better special education teacher, and I gained valuable leadership skills that would eventually aid me once I transitioned to administration.

Yes, I followed Mr. Johnson's advice, but not on purpose mind you. It was sort of by happen stance. My position as the SST Chair ended when we got a new principal, and she got the memo that it was a conflict of interest for a special education teacher to also chair SST.

The bell rang, and a line of students conjugated outside my classroom door. In five minutes, I had recollected over my 10 year career in education. Having resigned my post as administrator over the special education department the year before and only being back in the classroom for one year, I realized it was time for another transition. I had come off of a 12 week maternity leave, and Christmas break was around the corner. I had made up in my mind that I would resign in January to focus more on my duties as a mom.

The time I took to be at home gave me great clarity about life and of the career I so loved. Education was never my first choice. It had chosen me. From the time I changed my major as a second semester 19 year old college freshmen, I knew that if I wasn't a special education teacher, I wouldn't be a teacher at all. So, what causes someone who knows without a shadow of a doubt she has been called to the field of education to up and quit?

My prospective may be a little different from most, and what I believe to be true may not work for everyone. Like our students, each of us is too individual to respond to a one-size-fit all approach. What works best for Ms. Daniel, the science teacher, may not work for Mr. Andrews, the history teacher. Just because we all have teaching as a career in common, we can't assume that one size does fits all when suggesting strategies to prevent or deal with teacher burnout.

What I do propose is that all teachers should have an ITP (Individualized Transition Plan). Like students in the special education program, teachers need to outline goals and coordinate a set of activities that will promote their movement up and down the "educational career ladder." We need a plan for "switching things up." Doing anything long enough the same way year after year with the same type of students under the ever changing constrains most teachers are force to work inside is enough to drive anyone mad. I am not talking about changing up lesson plans and teaching strategies from year to year. Those are things we do anyway. What we need to do is tap into our many gifts and talents; as teachers, we have many. We need to assign ourselves challenges that are uniquely suited to our capabilities and desires. We then have to be bold enough to implement the plan we make. It's easy to identify a plan, but it's a whole other animal to leave our comfort zone to make that plan a reality.

Within the 10 years I taught, I had four different titles and worked with three different groups of students who had distinct characteristics. None of those titles took me totally out of the area I so love. That's what kept my career as a special education teacher fresh and exciting. I encountered the type of frustration that leads one to quit only when I got to a point of needing change, and I didn't have the next transition fall into my lap like before.

To be honest, my burnout didn't come from the massive paperwork I had to do as a teacher and administrator. Don't get me wrong; I hated the paperwork, but that came with the job. The long hours I spent at work didn't cause me to get to my place of burnout. I put in long hours with each of the titles that I had. It was an expectation I had of myself so that I could do the job I was doing to the best of my ability. My burnout wasn't even caused by the many changes and unrealistic expectations of administrators, or the bureaucracy of a school system. The burnout that I experienced may have been outgrowths of these things, but it wasn't the root.

As teachers, we need to be challenged. Not the challenge of doing more with less that many like to put on our shoulders, but a challenge that comes from ourselves to grow our talents and abilities. This could mean teaching a new discipline or new grade of students. For some, it may mean adding something like becoming a coach or advisor of an extracurricular activity. It may mean taking an educational sabbatical, moving up into administration or back into the classroom. The point is to "switch things up." The possibilities are endless and as varied as our individual differences.

After two years of being a stay-at-home mom, I am starting to feel burnout. I just can't quit on my wonderful little angel who is experiencing the "terrific twos." No I just have to consult my ITP, which is to transition back into the field I love. Not the way that it was, but as founder and director of the non-profit organization that I founded to mentor students with disabilities, speak on the issues affecting them, and eventually opening a school for students with disabilities. I think that is enough to keep me excited and engaged for the next 10 years. As for my little angel, well she has an ITP of her own. She will be transitioning into daycare. Like soon!

As for you, you are too valuable to lose. You still have too much to offer and impart to young minds. Develop your Individualized Transition Plan today and be courageous enough to implement it.

How to Develop an Individualized Transition Plan

When teachers become stagnant, we place ourselves at greater risk of burning out and for some ultimately leaving the profession. A transitional plan is critical to the longevity of your career in the field of education. Although there is no right way to develop a transition plan or template for writing one, there are certain things that every plan should include. I encourage you to think about what your plan will look like, create and implement it. I believe this is one way to avoid teacher burnout or at the least to prolong the inevitable.

1. **Conduct an interest inventory of the different aspects and positions related to your certification or areas you wish to be certified in**. Think about different subjects you can teach, sports that you can coach and organizations you could advise. Think about your gifts and talents, and how they can be used to enhance what you do now or could do in the future. Can you see yourself in administration at some point and/or teaching different grade levels? Now, make a list of all the different positions and titles you could possibly have throughout your tenure in the field of education.

2. **Write out the strategy you will adopt in order to transition into the areas you listed above.** Write in detail what is needed to be able to successfully transition into doing those things. For example, you may have an interest in being an ESOL teacher. You could research the qualifications, and your strategy to actually get certified to be an ESOL teacher would be to take one summer and complete the necessary coursework. Another example could be for someone interested in becoming a principal. Your strategy could include taking the necessary classes to obtain certification and even speaking with your principal to let him/her know of your interest. Ask if you could shadow him/her during your planning from time to time. You just might be surprised at

how much your principal will let you in on now that he/she knows you are also interested in leadership.

3. **Now that you are informed and have a strategy for implementation, create a timeline.** Include dates for when you would like to transition into doing the things you've listed. Depending on what you are transitioning into, this can be two to even five years out. The important thing is to assign a date. It can always be altered later if need be.

4. **Outline the benefits and downfalls involved in making that transition.** Some transitions may cause you a decrease in pay while others will be an increase. Other transitions may cause you to work with children while other transitions may put you in a position where you are working with only other adults. Write out how you will address any downfalls. For example, some transitions could take you away from working with students, which you love. In order to address that, you could coach a sport or become the adult advisor to an organization at your school.

5. **Review your plan.** Now that you have a picture of what other transitions you can make, the time frame in which you will or want to make them, and the benefits and downfalls of each, decide if it's worth it to do those things. If you decide it's not worth it, then simply take that part out and keep what is left.

6. **Implementation is the key, work your plan.** Be sure to review your plan at least yearly, but as often as you need to in order to get you to where you want to be.

Chapter 7

The Faces of Education

By: Lori H. Rice

Education has become about 'the numbers': Students on grade level, students at proficiency, the number of males performing at proficiency in reading, the number of females with advanced skills in mathematics. The list goes on and on. If you ask a teacher, not a single one will tell you they chose education as a profession because they like numbers, statistics or test scores. The burnout that often comes with the impersonal side of teaching can fade away when we stop and reflect on the faces of education right in front of our eyes.

We have many faces in our classrooms. Our students come to us from various backgrounds and experiences. They each bring something to our classrooms, something of themselves and their families that intertwines with who we are as a teacher. We learn and grow and become better from our experiences with each student. Positive or negative, good or bad, we keep part of them with us after they move on beyond our classroom doors.

Some of the faces in our classrooms come from struggling homes. Sam* was smaller than his classmates in size, but had enough self-esteem to overflow a room. This shaggy haired little boy came to my first grade classroom each day full of energy. He read any book I put in his hands, asked questions to my exhaustion, helped classmates even if he was not done with an activity, and bubbled over with a love of learning. I did not find a subject he didn't like. Sam soaked up every bit of knowledge I could provide for him and begged for more. His smile was contagious and held a spark of mischief every time he shared it, which was often. When we had a long break off school, Sam would always complain, "I don't want to stay home. I want to come to school." His single mother was doing the best she could to provide for a family, and Sam found his second home in my classroom.

Some of the faces in our classrooms come with labels. Pat* was gangly and thin with too much energy and creativity for one tiny body to hold. He had glasses that were always just a slight bit askew and forever smudged. He was far from a traditional student who learns and transfers information easily, asks questions, sits and raises his hand, and takes turns. Organization was a foreign word for this creative mind. Social skills were difficult as evidenced in interactions with peers or adults. He was known for violent outbursts and challenging authority. I met his challenges with steady respect and firm expectations. We found a rhythm in the learning and sharing of knowledge that happened in the classroom. He learned ways to interact with peers, offer assistance to others, and participate in our classroom community. I watched this brilliant and creative mind blossom and become comfortable within his body. Pat found peer acceptance in my classroom.

Some of the faces in our classroom come from sadness. Emma* was with me for a brief month. I remember her huge, beautiful, eyes staring blindly ahead, and her long straight hair always needing to be brushed. She kept to herself and was a quiet presence in our room. Reading her file was heartbreaking, and I was shocked to read her history. I felt immediate love for this small, fragile little girl. She was quiet and observing in my room. With a soft hand and respected space, she quietly worked and grew. Then one day she was gone. Emma found love in my classroom even if just for the briefest of moments.

Some of the faces in our classroom come from hospitals. Olivia* was out of class for a month in a children's hospital. She dealt with doctors and ICU, tubes and medicine, surgery and sickness. She was quiet and shy, but with a personality that fought to disprove those traits. She watched and followed. With space and care, Olivia slowly bloomed into a leader. Her personality surpassed her learning, and she morphed into an amazing, positive creature. Olivia found confidence in my classroom.

Some of the faces in our classroom come from working homes that can often be empty at the end of a school day. Matt* had a mom and dad and older siblings who loved him. He was the baby. With soft blonde hair and a smile to light the world, he loved school. He worked hard, sat quietly, and did what he could to participate in the classroom in every way. I could see the heart in this child from the first day of school. The students were coloring, using their new crayons, and his neighbor could not find a red. Without missing a beat, Matt took the red crayon he was coloring with, broke it quickly in half, handed half to his new friend, and said, "There! Now you have a red!" Matt found many friends in my classroom.

Some of the faces in our classroom come from learning. Their homes are full of books and board games with nightly dinner conversations and regular outings. Ali* had family members in education. She came to me a student. She knew how to take turns, how to work independently, how to read, and the inner workings of a classroom environment. Her beautiful brown eyes were always taking in everything. She observed what others were learning and the questions they were asking. With patience and prompting as I asked her many, many questions, she drew upon her own strength and began to take control of her learning. Her smile became even brighter. Ali became a problem solver in my classroom.

There are more. Each face in our classroom is an individual with a story and a purpose, joy and sadness. They are not numbers, never numbers. These faces are our future doctors, lawyers, citizens, workers, scientists, business people, idea creators and leaders. These faces will provide the solutions to our world's challenges and move the world in ways we do not even know possible right now. When you hear the newest statistics in education, know they are not numbers.

Reflect on your students. Remember those you have had successes with and learn from those you have not. They are the driving force in your learning, your lessons, and your classroom. These are the faces of education.

*Names have been changed.

Chapter 8

What If Your Boss is an Idiot?

By: Jania Hoover

Disclaimer: These stories are all true; however, they do not all relate to one particular principal. Some of these vignettes relate to experiences I've had while others relate to stories I've heard.

A major factor affecting teacher burnout is the lack of supportive administration. But what if you work for an idiot? There is no worse feeling than to go to work every day feeling like the boss you work for and policies you have to follow are ill-advised, asinine, and just flat-out stupid.

It's one thing when you work in a regular 9-5 job, and your boss gets on your nerves. In a school, every single decision affects the lives of countless children. Many leaders in schools have absolutely no concept of reality when it comes to the truth of the classroom. It's like they teach just long enough to get a position as an administrator, and then completely forget what it is like to be a classroom teacher.

It's extremely hard to follow someone when you don't agree with their vision. It's even worse when you have no idea what the vision is. To make it more tolerable to work for an idiot, I present the following ten strategies:

1. **Limit your interaction with your principal.** I have found that my frustration levels increased exponentially during staff meetings and other times I had to interact with the principal. For my own sanity, I avoided talking with the principal unless it was absolutely necessary. I did my best to remain cordial when I had to deal with the principal but I avoided non-essential interaction. When you don't respect the leader, just stay away from him/her. Go to work, do your job, teach your kids. You don't have to be in the principal's face in order to do a good job in your classroom. Don't ignore direct requests, of course, however, when you don't have to speak to your principal—don't.

2. **<u>Don't let his/her power trip get too far under your skin</u>.** I had to learn that some people need to justify their existence as a leader. They do this by disrespecting the people they are supposed to lead. They also do this by lording their position over the heads of those they supervise. I learned this lesson when I missed a mandatory after-hours school activity. My family had come in town for my graduation. My family lives in 4 different states, and we don't get together often. My school had its Achievement Ceremony on the last night my brothers were in town. I decided to miss the ceremony so I could spend time with them. I emailed the principal to let him know I'd be missing the event to spend time with my family. His response: "That is not an acceptable excuse, but I will accept it." I will admit I was beyond upset and had the full intention of giving that principal a piece of my mind. Thankfully, cooler heads prevailed. I closed that email and realized something. This was a person that needed to feel better about himself by asserting authority over those he perceived to be of lesser value than himself. Once that realization smacked me in the face, it was much easier to deal with him as well as other supervisors/administrators that had not possessed many good leadership qualities. Some of those who have leadership positions let the titles give them extreme delusions of grandeur. They lord their positions over those they supervise and seem to get a thrill from forcing them to submit to their will. I do not respond well to power

trips, but thankfully I've always been able to remember *their* power trip is not *my* problem.

3. **Bite your tongue.** Another strategy I employ when working for idiots is to bite my tongue. It is very hard for me to hide my feelings, but I am very careful to keep my words focused on issues, and not how stupid I perceive that person to be. I have absolutely no poker face though, but as long as the principal doesn't look at me when he's talking, he will never know how stupid I think he is.

   Pick your battles VERY carefully. I do not fight every policy that doesn't make sense to me (there are too many of those). I choose instead to focus only on those that absolutely demand my attention. I've had principals that nitpick on the most minor of non-academic tasks. One principal wrote a comment on my observation for me to write my agenda on one side of the board. (I had it split because I taught 2 classes and there was a big Promethean board in the middle of my board.) There was another time when the principal told the staff they needed to write 2 activities in every portion of the lesson plan. He asked for two activities in the opening, two in the work session, and two in the closing. There was a ten minute discussion about why a 'ticket out the door' was not an effective closing. I wanted to pull my hair out. No matter how annoyed I was with the entire discussion, I held my tongue.

4. **Give them what they want- no matter how ridiculous it seems.** A coworker sounded panicked as she tried to understand why she needed to write two activities on the board. I tapped her on her shoulder and said, "Just write two things on the board." She said, "But what else do I do if a ticket out the door isn't enough?" I shook my head and repeated myself, "Just WRITE two things on the board." To save her sanity and that of everyone else in the meeting, I got her to understand my point.

When you're dealing with a micro-manager, sometimes you just have to give them what they want. I wrote two things on each section on my board. That had absolutely no bearing on what I actually did in my classroom. Instead of trying to make my principal drop his ridiculous two-activity requirement, I just followed it. *Give the principal what s/he wants.* The principal rarely came into my room anyway. I wasn't willing to fight a battle over writing insignificant information on my board. In my school, the information on the board is for the visitors to my classroom more than for the students themselves. Although I had no clue why the principal spent twelve minutes discussing why he wanted teachers to write two tasks on each section of the board, I did not say anything. In the grand scheme of things, what I write on my board has no bearing on how I teach my kids. So I gave him what he wanted. I've had a principal that gave constant last minute instructions that made absolutely no sense. I've had principals that change policies as often as they change their clothes. As long as it doesn't go too far against what I am able to tolerate, I do what I'm told.

5. **Stick to your core beliefs.** I have no problem giving a principal what s/he wants, as long as it doesn't go too far against what I believe about education. However, I am a fan of the tried and true practice of 'closing my door and teaching.' No matter what the principal asks me to do, I am the expert when it comes to my kids and my content. I have to be the one to make the ultimate decisions when it comes to what I do in my classroom. I will consider what the principal asks me to do, but when it goes too far from what I know to be right, I go with my gut.

   I use standards-based grading practices in my classroom. I've learned a lot about assessment and grading over my eight years in the classroom, and I've completely changed how I assign grades to my students. My policies don't mesh well with traditional grading procedures, and I've had three principals challenge me about them. I dig my heels on my grading policies more often than not because what I'm doing is right. Were these principals less clueless, I would have shared some of the research and statistics with them. I never wasted my time on that task. I learned long ago not to argue with fools--from far away you can't tell who is who.

6. **Speak Up.** When there is a situation that demands your attention, don't bite your tongue. Sometimes you have to directly challenge policies/procedures that don't make sense. Early in my teaching career, the principal made the decision to have three teachers teach US history. These teachers would also teach one or two other subjects. It did not make sense to take the most heavily-tested course to be diluted among three different teachers. It would have been easy to have two teachers teach it, having one teach only US history and the other teach US history and one other subject. I spoke to my department chair about this, and we spoke with the principal. He responded that teachers should 'be flexible.' He didn't change the schedule. When test scores plummeted, he asked me what happened. When I mentioned the schedule, he said, "Well, why didn't you say anything beforehand?"

   I'm not always unsuccessful when I speak up. My grade-level team and I decided it would be helpful to have a conference day for our students; we brought it to the principal, we made our case and he gave his approval. Other times, I speak up to ask questions for clarification. I often meet teachers that are afraid to challenge anything the principal says or does. I would argue that it is not what you say, but how you say it that can cause or mitigate a conflict.

7. **Prioritize based on what 'they' say you HAVE to do, and what you know is important.** Working for an idiot burns teachers out because they are often pulled in so many

competing directions. In one week, I was told to assign writing assignments once a week, to assign writing assignments once every 6 weeks, to hold on to said writing assignments and to turn them in once a week. Could you follow that? Me neither. I prioritize my to-do lists based on what absolutely, positively HAS to be done. That means, I typically don't do something the first time the principal says it needs to be done. I figure, if the principal says it two or three times, and establishes a deadline, then I will do it. It's easy for a teacher to get burned out just by thinking of the sheer volume of tasks that demand attention on a daily basis.

Prioritization is KEY. Remember, your first priority is to teach your kids. Everything else comes secondary. Find strategies that help you manage what HAS to be done without losing your mind. I have a coworker that ignores emails. He said he gets more done when he doesn't check them. He's established a system that works for him. Develop a system that works for you.

8. **Create a support system.** I can't count the amount of times I've shaken my head or furrowed my brow at something the principal has said or done. At the end of the day, I work for my kids, not the principal. If the principal is not on my side, that means he is not on the side of the kids either. I am there to teach. I close my door, and I teach my kids. No matter how frustrating the principal can be at times, as long as

you're at that school, you have to be the best teacher you can be.

Any teacher will need a support system, but it's even more crucial when you're working for an idiot. Make 'work friends'. It's okay if you don't hang out with these people outside of work. However, you need friendly faces to help you make it through the day. The worst thing you can do is isolate yourself from the staff. There will often be at least a few people that feel exactly the way you do about the principal. They can help you determine what is mandatory and which policies are not. They can tell you the best place to go for happy hour. Your support system makes your situation bearable.

9. **Close your door and teach.** You got into teaching for a reason. I guarantee it wasn't to let a stupid principal douse your fire. Remember why you began teaching and try your best to find ways to remind yourself of that every day. Connect with your students. Find ways to share your passion about your content area with them. Find a way to laugh every day. Start a notebook where you write down the things that make you happy about your job. When you look at the good things, it makes it easier to deal with the idiot that is your boss.

10. **Leave work at work.** I learned this lesson the hard way. I became SO frustrated with my job that it was consuming my

thoughts even when I wasn't at work. I had to establish some boundaries quickly. I decided that my home would be my happy space. I do not, under any circumstances, bring work home. Before I made this rule, I would bring stacks of paper home to grade and I would bring the same bag (still not graded) back to work the next day. Even worse, I would get a headache just thinking of the fact that I needed to grade those assignments. I want my home to be my place of serenity, so it is now a 'No-Work Zone'.

In addition, I accepted a long time ago that I will NEVER finish everything that NEEDS to be done. I get to work when I need to be there, and I don't stay longer than my contracted hours. Anything that doesn't get done within those hours will have to wait until the next day. I've had principals that ask me to do things outside school hours (with no compensation), and try to guilt trip me by saying 'it's for the kids.' That used to work during my first couple of years, but not anymore. I have no problem going above and beyond when I actually respect my boss and understand the school's vision. When I don't, it is imperative for me to spend as little time in the school building as possible. This means I have to get creative about getting things done. This means writing lesson plans during lunch, advisory (homeroom), or during student 'independent work sessions'. This means, establishing a schedule of after-school tutorial, instead of being available for students to drop in on any day.

Hopefully you never have to work for an idiot. However, my anecdotal evidence tells me that most teachers will at some point work with a principal that is grossly under-qualified for the job. Use these tips to make your experience more worthwhile. And don't forget, the principal will most likely be gone before you are!

Chapter 9

I Was DONE!

By: Franchesca Warren

I was DONE. D-O-N-E. After being in the classroom eleven years, I was tired of the politics, the 'top down' policies, and years of not getting a pay raise. As I looked at everything I was going through the only possibility I could see was me typing my resignation letter and finding other employment. So one evening, I sat in my office and typed up my resignation letter. It went like this:

Dear Mrs. Sloan,

I, Franchesca Warren, am resigning from my job as a teacher at Anywhere High School. My last day will be May 31st.

It was short, sweet and went right to the point I had tried to convey for the last six months. However, instead of immediately turning the letter in, I put it in my purse so that I could turn it in 'at the right time.' There were days that went by where I was on the verge of turning it in, but then something always stopped me and told me to wait--my time would come.

For weeks this resignation letter went everywhere I went. Because we were so close to Spring Break, I decided that I would stop procrastinating and turn it in the Friday before Spring Break, so that there would not be a lot of discussion from my principal about why I was not coming back the next year.

All the while I kept my letter a secret from my friends and co-workers because I didn't want to answer questions like: How would I make money? What was I going to do in my spare time? How would I take care of my family? Not because I didn't *want* to answer them, but because I *couldn't* -- I didn't know myself.

On the Friday before Spring Break, I got sick and had to go home early-causing me to totally forget about the letter in my purse. So during the week of Spring Break, I decided to just relax and figure out what my next steps were. One day I went to the mall, and as I was exiting my favorite shoe shop I heard someone call my name. "Ms. Lane!" I turned around saw one of my former students, Felecia grinning at me. Felecia was one of more difficult students I'd ever taught. She constantly disrupted class, fought and even (at times) was disrespectful to the entire class. Through my constant contact with her father and her long weekends on Saturday Detention, by the time she graduated she was well on her way to college.

We talked for about 10 minutes and right before we parted she told me, "Your class changed my life. Thank you for all you did for me." After our meeting, all I could think about was students like her. Students, who struggled in my class, but due to my constant redirection, actually came out better students. I thought about all the hundreds of students who came through my doors that I had similar experiences with. As I continued to ponder the letter (that was still in my purse), something in me told me my time was not up in the classroom-not yet.

By the time school started back, I had torn up my letter that was in my purse but only because I loved the work I was able to do with the kids. But just like my wish to stay was strong, I knew I couldn't do things that I had done in the past. Things were going to have to change. As I walked into my classroom fresh from Spring Break an idea 'hit' me. I was going to do something radical. In an effort to keep my teaching 'about the kids' and no one else, I decided to shut my door and just teach.

That's right. I would not do anything else unless it was about the kids. I didn't want to serve on any more committees or do any work that did not directly impact the kids. Instead, I would come to work every day, teach my heart out and then go home at the end of the day. I wouldn't let policies that obviously did not help the kids get me stressed out so that I couldn't perform in the classroom. How hard could this be?

My first test came about two weeks after Spring Break when my principal wanted to do some late ‘test prep’ for the state exams. Her plan was to pull identified kids out of their classes and after school every day leading to the test until 6 pm. In an effort to get teachers ‘on board' with her plan, my principal individually went to each teacher in my department to gain their approval. When she came to me, I listened intently and then politely declined the after school option. I had kids. There was no way I could stay at school for 12 hours. Flabbergasted by my finality, she implored to know what was ‘wrong with me.' I tried to explain to her my reasoning, but she wasn't hearing it. Finally she told me that she ‘respected' my decision and left me alone.

I had stood up for what I said I was going to do, and now something told me that the last 8 weeks would be difficult for me but I didn't care. Instead, I decided to take my new mantras through the end of the year (and summer) to refresh me in my craft. I did the following actions:

1. **<u>I focused only on teaching and learning in my classroom.</u>** This was hard at first because I had been an integral part of my school for so long. I was a sponsor of a sport, ran several clubs and even stayed after school every day to finish up on my work. However, by me putting so much energy on things that were not in the classroom, it was effecting me inside the classroom. I was mentally exhausted and many times I only ‘half did’ things inside my classroom.

The moment that I started to focus ONLY on teaching and learning was the moment that everything changed. I became energized all over again with the possibilities of the things I could do for my students!

2. **I made sure that I took time for me to develop as a professional.** Instead of dreading professional development, I began to volunteer to 'lead' training for the staff. Leading trainings helped me help other teachers who were struggling in areas that I was excelling in. In addition, this allowed me to make great professional contacts. In addition to leading professional development, I also began to research various professional development opportunities in my area. I was stunned at all of the (good) PD I never knew about! I even developed my own professional development plan to help strengthen me as a professional.

3. **I refused to work on any programs during the summer.** Every year since I started teaching I had worked summer programs instead of using that time to 'reenergize' for the upcoming year. However, last summer I decided to not work at all during the summer. Instead, I used this time to attend Professional Development and just relax. Needless to say, by the time I came back to school, I was reenergized to teach!

By the time the end of the year came I felt refreshed, and with my time off during the summer, I really began to enjoy my job again.

I thought I was done with teaching but really this was only the beginning!

Chapter 10

F. I. G. M. O.
Forget It, I've Got My Orders

By: Jania Hoover

When a teacher is burned out, when they just can't take it anymore, they just may get to F.I.G.M.O status. You find yourself doing these things:

- Counting down from Friday to Friday, and from break to break.

- Depression sets in on Sunday at the thought of returning to your classroom for another week.
- When you schedule elective surgeries so you can miss school.
- When you get in a minor car accident, and you're happy because it means you can miss work for a few days.
- When you wish for the flu so you don't have to come to work.

If you are experiencing these things, it just MAY be time to move on.

F. I. G. M. O. is an acronym I learned from my military family members. It stands for "Forget it, I've got my orders." It means that, once you've received your "orders," or you've decided to leave, you shouldn't let the bad parts of the job get to you anymore.

When your dislike of your job starts to take a physical toll on you, it's time to go. I found myself having trouble sleeping, plagued by massive headaches, and withdrawn from normal activities. I had to make a change. I had no idea what to do, but I knew that I had to do something different. I was absolutely no good for myself, and I definitely was no good for my kids. I even went to a psychologist. I felt like I was on the verge of a breakdown. When I left that doctor's office, I knew I had to leave my job. I didn't know what I would do next, but I knew I could not stay at that school a minute longer.

If you still don't know what F.I.G.M.O looks like, see if any of these symptoms sound familiar:

- Do you say no when anyone asks you to do anything outside of school hours?

- Do you get to school at the last possible second and leave as soon as possible after school?
- Do you complete the mandatory tasks you are asked to complete and ignore the rest?
- Do you get a headache as soon as you walk into the school that disappears when the final bell rings?
- Do you take time off for 'mental health' days, just because?

The worst thing a teacher can do is stay in the classroom past his/her expiration date. If you have tried over and over again, to deal with the chaos in your schoolhouse and nothing changes, it's time to do something different. The kids do not deserve a 'half-ass teacher'. If you can't be effective anymore, you need to leave. If you don't even want to try anymore, it's time to move on.

This is not a decision to take lightly. I was frustrated for YEARS before I got to the point when I was strong enough to demand a change for myself. We all know the statistics of teachers leaving the classroom. I know tons of people that tell me, "I used to teach". I truly feel like this is my calling, so even though I was having these issues, I knew that I didn't want to leave education altogether. There are a variety of paths you can take when you get to "F.I.G.M.O" status. That being said, I knew that I couldn't remain in my current situation.

Here are some questions to ask when you're at the end of your rope:

1. Do I still want to teach?
2. Do I still want to teach here?
3. What exactly do I dislike about this position?

4. What exactly do I like about this position?
5. What will I do if I don't work here?
6. What would make this job bearable?
7. If I can't change my situation, can I change my outlook about my current job situation?
8. What would make me happy in terms of my job?
9. Do I need a change of scenery?
10. Do I need to leave the classroom?
11. Should I go back to school for an additional endorsement/degree/certification?
12. Do I need a break?

Only you can decide when enough is enough. Once you get to that point, you must make a change. Once you know it's time to go, no need to let little things get to you…you can just say: F.I.G.M.O!

Chapter 11

Get Out of There!

By: Cari Harris

The best advice I ever received about how to be a good teacher was to make sure you stop teaching. Not forever – just every so often, and for longer than a summer. The advice came from my mentor when I was a student teacher. I was so passionate and ready to begin my second career as a high school teacher, but I also knew I needed to learn on the job from a master. My mentor was definitely a master. He had taught for almost 30 years, and he had lost neither his passion nor his ability to try new ideas and learn new things. How did he do it, I wondered? His secret wasn't about choosing brilliant curriculums, planning dynamic lessons, or even creating fun assessments. No, his secret to keeping his passion for the classroom: every 8 to 10 years, he purposely stopped teaching for at least a year.

More than most careers, teaching has the potential to lead quickly to burnout. The average teacher leaves the profession after only 5 years. As a new teacher, I couldn't imagine getting tired of it; I was so excited to finally have my own classroom! Yes, school is often the place of our greatest joys and triumphs, it is the place where we practice our expertise, and we reach the students we care so much about. A classroom can be one of the gifts of education: our own space to create the kind of learning environment for our students that we hoped for. But it's that very classroom that can often wrap us in a blanket of isolation, stress and obligation. If we aren't careful, the endless meetings, the long hours of planning, the frustration of mandates, lack of resources and overcrowded rooms can push us onto the fast track towards burnout.

The school I trained in, and ended up teaching in for the next seven years, was a huge, urban school. My mentor hadn't taught in those halcyon (and imaginary) days of 20 students in a class, jaunty letterman sweaters and college bound students. He'd been in that school for decades, struggling year after year to create that learning space in lean times as well as times of respite. But what really allowed him to maintain his passion for the classroom, he told me early on, was that he took a break and left town for at least a year. The practice of taking a sabbatical has sadly gone out of style for most teachers. It used to be the practice of many professional educators – and was encouraged by administrators – to take a year or two away from their school to further their own education or experiences.

The idea behind the sabbatical is to take that well-deserved and much needed break from the classroom in order to engage in furthering your own expertise. You might engage in research, get a new degree or certification, travel on an exchange experience, or take part in a practicum in another academic arena. Growing as experts in our field is an important side of maintaining our effectiveness as teachers – but that doesn't only happen in our own classroom or during required professional development seminars.

Because most teachers leave the career field in as few as five years, thinking about sabbaticals within three years of starting in the profession is not out of the question. If you have already been teaching for longer than half a decade, it's time to start planning that sabbatical now! Just knowing that you will be taking a break may give you the boost you need to survive whatever stresses you are currently facing.

There are some important things to remember about planning a sabbatical, so it's good to be thoughtful once you decide to plan one:

1. **Don't wait until you're already burned out and over-stressed.** It's easy to just keep "pushing through the pain" of the initial feelings of burn-out, but you do yourself no

favors by ignoring your increased tiredness and stress. Planning ahead before the burnout gives you clear-thinking moments to plan something that will make your time away from the classroom truly rejuvenating and productive.

2. **Consider how long you'd like your sabbatical to last.** What would you like to do? If you want to pursue a new academic degree, will it take you one or two years? How much time might you need for travel? Will you be away from your home? Don't let questions like this keep you from planning a sabbatical. Instead, look at them as steps to renewal! One way I learned about opportunities was to take short term opportunities to attend conferences or seminars in subject areas I was interested in. Going to a weekend conference could produce a networking opportunity that could lead you to a very rewarding sabbatical.

3. **Plan your finances.** Look into your contract or the policy of your school or district about sabbaticals. Most contracts will hold your position for you up to two years, and some even provide funding for various types of out-of-classroom work. You don't want to struggle financially the year that you are on sabbatical, so you want to have the time to plan how you will support yourself during that time away. One thing I found were numerous grants and scholarships that supported teachers in my subject area, and obtaining one of

those had a huge impact on my consideration of what kind of sabbatical I might consider.

4. **<u>Your sabbatical away from the school does not mean that you have to leave town!</u>** You may decide to pursue an online degree, which allows you to take a break from teaching, but not have to uproot yourself from your daily life. You may decide to take on a role as a TOSA (Teacher On Special Assignment) where you can serve in a different capacity in your own or another district. You may decide to combine some education opportunities with a new roll within your community or local government. There are all kinds of possibilities that don't require you to leave town. Think about the direction you'd like to take for your career, the areas of expertise you'd like to expand into, and brainstorm all the amazing possibilities!

5. **<u>ENJOY your sabbatical!</u>** The point is to refresh your outlook, lessen your stress, and regain your energy and passion for education. Finding balance again and joy in not only your career choice as a teacher, but in life in general, is a huge and important gift you can give yourself.

My mentor teacher took his first sabbatical during his tenth year of teaching. He joined the Peace Corps and taught in Romania for two years. It was a challenging and awesome experience for him, and one he drew upon for the rest of his career. He took his second sabbatical nine years later when he decided to take a year to obtain a master's degree in criminal justice – just because that area of study interested him (not to mention made him even more of an expert in his teaching area of government and civics). He was a better teacher for those experiences, and by the time I met him, in his 28th year of teaching, he was still as passionate, invested in, and excited about his work.

My mentor teacher had created realistic boundaries for himself and had learned that he valued his career, his students and his colleagues so much more for having taken regular breaks from them. It was the best example of managing a robust teaching career that I could have asked for. I have always interspersed my teaching career with taking opportunities to pursue new professional directions for myself. It made a huge difference for my perspective when I was in school. There are numerous ways for you to deal with teaching burnout. One of the best may be to simply get out of the classroom, just for a while.

Chapter 12

Trust the Gardener

By: Lori H. Rice

The main audience for this chapter is administration. If you are struggling and feel you need support from your administration, share this chapter with them. If you are in a leadership role in your Professional Learning Community, your team, or within your school or building, reflect on how you can use these key ideas to have a positive impact on teachers around you. We must turn to our experts in the field of education and support each other during these changing times in our profession.

Gardens can be created in many different sizes, shapes, combinations, and locations. Each school in our nation is like this. In gardening, there are landscaping jobs: nursery jobs, greenhouse jobs, botanical garden jobs, irrigation jobs. In schools there are administrative jobs, teaching jobs, secretarial jobs, bus drivers, food workers, and more. Each of these positions has purpose and needs the support of the others for the community to prosper and grow.

There are many types of administrators that touch the lives of students and teachers in our school systems. There a principals, assistant principals, curriculum directors, and superintendents. Their jobs have purpose, and we could not function as a working whole without everyone involved. I have had the good fortune of working for a strong leader, and I thank her for the leadership she provides. I also know there are other leaders elsewhere that are tired, worn down, power driven, weak, or simply not doing their job. Our schools should always have the children in the forefront. We need to become a culture where we work together for our future. With appreciation, tools, respect, and open minds we can accomplish this together.

I am not a gardener. I do, however, love looking at beautiful gardens, and I have found myself going to garden shows and wandering around, admiring the beauty of outdoor pavilions and rock gardens, waterfalls and ponds, flowers and a well landscaped lawn. I am able to keep a few plants alive in pots on my porch and patio. The flowers I plant in my flower garden, however, unfortunately never survive. Beyond that, I do not kid myself, and I don't attempt to maintain a well-manicured lawn. It is not realistic, and I leave that to the professionals. I trust those who have their hands in the dirt every day and know the business of creating and maintaining beauty in gardens.

Many times in life you have to know your limitations and trust those around you. Much like a beautiful landscaped garden, a school system is composed of many parts and elements. Each of these systems requires expertise and will prosper when it is tended correctly. The elements must work together as a whole unit to keep the system running, efficient, and prospering. Somewhere in our history as an American public educational system we lost sight of this. We have those in upper administrative or legislative roles giving advice and mandates to those of us with our hands in the dirt. If you want your garden to bloom and grow, you need to trust the systems to work in harmony.

Teachers are the experts in the classroom. They are experts in their grade level and content area. They know how to teach children and when we find a challenge, we read and research and ask experts about what we need to know. Teachers are constantly learning and finding new ideas and information. If you are struggling and find yourself in a negative environment, find ways you can ask for or get support. Pull on your strength and teach your administration and leaders what you need from them to function as an effective school to better serve the needs of the staff and students.

1. **It's dirty work.** Just as a gardener gets down in the dirt, so do teachers. We need administrators who appreciate all that

is being done. There are teachers who do this in the school building and are working until late at night. There are teachers who do this at home after their own families are tucked into bed. There are teachers that do this early in the morning before others start their day. Understand that what we do is often happening below the surface, much like the root structures and care that goes into maintaining a rich soil. Working in schools, Principals should appreciate this with verbal recognition and understanding when we (teachers) occasionally need time in leaving a few minutes early or arriving a few minutes late. These little acts show value for our time. Teachers can communicate with team leaders and administrators the need for understanding.

2. **The right tools get the job done.** A gardener uses trowels and shovels and water, teachers need books and technology and supplies. We need administrators who provide money and advocate for resources and help in our classrooms. Teachers are resourceful and creative. We find ways to provide many of the needs in our classrooms. We ask parents, we purchase items ourselves, and we are experts at finding free and repurposed resources. Having support from administrators shows respect for what we are implementing and doing in our classrooms. Teachers can advocate for supplies, explaining what tools are needed and the power of putting these tools in student's hands.

3. **<u>It takes time to grow.</u>** The beginning a seed develops underground where you cannot see the process, much of our students' growth happens inside too. We need administrators who see the big picture. Our classrooms are microenvironments. We create classrooms where students can trust and risk and fail and grow. Sometimes this is a slow process. There may appear to be times when we are stagnant, but there are so many valuable things going on with thinking and problem solving and learning. Showing understanding of learning and developing skills for lifelong learners takes trust. Respecting our culture of learning shows you trust the important work that is going on and will continue to go on after students leave our doors. Teachers can communicate with parents and administration the stages of learning and development so they understand stagnant times of growth.

4. **<u>There is beauty in each individual</u>**. A garden is composed of different varieties and species of flowers, plants, even insects to keep the garden healthy. Our schools are composed of unique individuals that work together for the whole community. We need administrators who understand differences. Just as we work to differentiate for students, so should the administrators differentiate for our teachers. We too learn in different ways, have different strengths, and have different weaknesses. We need administrators who support these differences and create a

culture where each of us feels worth and can therefore work together to form a beautiful bouquet.

Gardens can be created in many different sizes, shapes, combinations, and locations. Each school in our nation is like this. They are beautiful gardens with teachers doing their work in the classrooms to nurture students so they can grow and blossom. Administrators who can appreciate the work that goes into the classroom, find resources and tools necessary for the job to be done well, see the big picture and the whole student, and value the individuals that make up their school system are necessary. Teachers are the best advocates for individuals. Continue to speak up for your students, their needs, and what they are doing in your classroom.

Teachers get this. We are the gardener, deep in the work. We know we do valuable work, need tools for growing, teach deeper concepts that often need time to process, and see beauty in each individual. If you are blessed to have support from your administration, thank them for their work as well. My grandmother always said, "Treat others as you would like to be treated." If you are struggling with your administration, share this story with them. Provide a gentle reminder that we are all on the same path to stretch our students in their future. Lastly, be the voice for our children. Write to your legislature. Tell them the work you are doing. Tell them the support you need. Share your story.

We need administrators, those in control of funding, and our teaching staff working together to nurture these schools. We need the powers that be to understand we are all in this for the same cause, our children. We need to be trusted to do the jobs we were hired to do. We need people who trust the gardener to plant and nurture and grow the garden well. With appreciation, tools, respect, and open minds we can accomplish this together.

Chapter 13

Burning the Candle at Both Ends

By: Sarah J. Sorge

I have a hard time learning to say no. I don't want to inconvenience anyone, least of all my students or my colleagues. I feel a sense of moral obligation to be anything and everything that's asked of me, and this has been the norm for the entirety of my life.

As a teacher, saying no is even harder when I look at someone who desperately needs my help: the student who needs that college or scholarship recommendation at the last minute, the colleague who needs an extra chaperone at a dance, the principal that needs a faculty member to spearhead a new club or student organization… Have you ever found yourself smiling, saying "Sure! Whatever you need!" and then secretly wondering how you can make it all work out?

In college, I had a professor that once said, "Those who burn brightest, burn quickest." I never believed him, at least until I became a teacher. In my efforts to be everything I could be to my students, administration, and faculty, I often neglect myself and what I need, personally and professionally. I began to learn what it is to burn the candle at both ends, and occasionally how I could add an additional wick to the middle of my candle in order to accomplish more when I was already reaching my limit. In my efforts to burn brightly and distinguish myself as a reliable, exceptional teacher, I was burning myself out. I didn't hold myself as a priority when I should have, and I felt that if I did attempt to do something for myself, I was despicably selfish. I think this is the nature of who we are as educators; we are tirelessly selfless for the betterment of others. It's not in our job description, yet it is part of the fabric that makes us a unique career group. We give until we have nothing left, and even then we'll scrape the bottom of the metaphorical barrel in order to take up the last dregs so we won't see disappointment in the eyes of those around us.

Let me ask you, dear reader, when was the last time you did something for you? Go ahead; I'll wait. Give it a moment. If you cannot give me an answer with an almost knee-jerk reaction, I can safely tell you that you are not considering your own needs. Outside of school we are caregivers, parents, part-time workers, friends, counselors, chauffeurs… many hats for one person. It's not always easy to do it all, and burnout often seems to happen when someone is trying to take on too much too quickly. There is nothing wrong with taking time for yourself. There is no crime in deciding you want to go to a café after school to have a cup of coffee and enjoy the silence. You are not a traitor if you decide to meet the guys for wing night on Friday night while you watch the game. I promise it will be okay. No one will think less of you; in fact, some might ask why it took you so long.

It is also perfectly fine to say you need help. Think about it this way: you are so reliable that your colleagues and administration come to you when they get into a bind and need help. You should not perceive yourself as different from them. You are not a lesser person if you need to put the "paddle in the air"; if you are in distress, you can ask a colleague if they can cover the dance for you or if someone else could run the concession stand at the basketball game. While I understand that we, as teachers, have many responsibilities (contractual or otherwise), you have to make your needs a priority. Make a promise to yourself today. I will make myself a priority. Repeat it; make it part of your daily alarm to remind you to say that to yourself. You can do small things like giving yourself 15 minutes or so to write in a journal (which could help you sort out why you are specifically feeling burnt out), go to see a movie after work, play a short game of pickup basketball with your friends, get a manicure-do whatever it takes to relax.

The ways to deal with burnout are as multi-varied and multifaceted as the teacher who is experiencing it; therefore, what works for one teacher may not work for another. I know one teacher who finds it incredibly relaxing to be in her garden planting and weeding. That is not my way to relax; the mere idea of weeding and mulching is enough to send me running to the next town! However, a relaxed teacher is an effective teacher. You are your best as a teacher when you are giving your all, and you cannot do that if you are thinking about the mile-long list of things you have to do.

My next bit of advice is to take some of your volunteered responsibilities and mark them “return to sender.” I had to stop teaching religious education several years ago because I was so exhausted with lesson plans and writing my Master’s thesis that Sunday became my only day to actually sleep in and get a little rest. I still volunteer when they ask me, but I now have the ability to pick and choose based on my own schedule and needs. You can ask for additional help if you still want to make a particular responsibility a priority; at least some of the weight will be lifted off of you.

Finally, learn that it's ok to say no! There will come a point when you realize there just aren't enough hours in the day to accomplish what you need. Be tactful, be courteous, and you'll generally find that people are very open to helping as much as they can.

Sometimes they do not know just how much work you have, which is an innocent mistake. You can say something to the tune of: "I wish I could help, but I have a lot to do already," or "Sorry, I have other commitments that interfere with..." among others. Normally, the person asking will be very open to that; they're human too and realize we all have limits.

You are worth every moment you give yourself. Go for it! Blow out a couple flames on your "candle" so you can shine brightly and efficiently.

Chapter 14

A Reduction in Force

By: Franchesca Warren

"I can't believe I'm here." That's all I kept saying as I stood in line with hundreds of other teachers to reapply for our jobs. Here I was, a veteran teacher with multiple degrees and a wide range of experience, yet due to a reduction in force within my school district my entire career was in jeopardy. As I looked around the room, I saw teachers young and old walking around like they were shell shocked at the possibility of not having a job due to no fault of their own.

Yes, the school year had been difficult and I had even questioned if I would return in the upcoming Fall, but standing in line trying to give my resume to potential principals made me realize that not only did I need to be in the classroom, but I couldn't picture me leaving education. But that decision was no longer in my hands. My professional life depended on if I found a principal that needed my position. So, I went home and waited for my fate.

All evening the thoughts of not having a job made me even more depressed. Going back to work the next day wasn't any help because everyone was almost hysterical. Many of my co-workers already had 'back up' plans in case their positions didn't get renewed. My principal tried to calm our fears, but honestly he couldn't tell us what he didn't know so we waited. For the next couple of weeks, this was what life was like for everyone in my school. A shell-shocked experience.

As I sat and tried to grade some papers on my planning period, I had an epiphany. Why was I depending on a school district for my livelihood as an educator? I was an educator, and it didn't matter if I got a contract or not. My mission in life was to help children. The longer I thought, the angrier I became. However, after each thought of anger, the same question came to me.

So what are you going to do about it? How are you going to make a difference? These thoughts stayed with me for months, until***I*** decided that ***I*** would change how teachers were viewed by the public. Yes, I was just a teacher but being a teacher meant that I was an expert about all things that happened in education. I didn't need to conduct studies; I was on the 'front lines' already. So I decided to create a forum that would give teachers a voice. I decided to create a forum where teachers would be celebrated and never made to feel incompetent or unworthy of professionalism. On that day The Educator's Room, the first online magazine for educators by educators, was born. As I awaited word on my position, I poured all of my energy into making The Educator's Room a reality. On August 1st, 2012, my dream became a reality.

In the end, I received a contract to be able to teach my beloved students for another year, and I found another passion- fighting to help teachers who were like me- burnt out.

Afterword

By: Lori H. Rice

Our world is ever changing. I can just imagine the one room school house teacher filling the stove with the firewood she hauled in, cleaning the chalkboard, and looking through piles of slates thinking, "It sure would be nice to have someone to collaborate with." I know when I first started teaching there were many schools and classrooms that taught based on textbooks, what they wanted, what was "fun", and what they thought was right. I know I was thinking, "It sure would be nice to have a guide for what to teach." And here we are today with technology, inclusion, differentiation and we think, "It sure would be nice if…." Our world is ever changing.

We as educators are on a journey to touch the future. This work is hard. This work is tiring. This work is thankless. IF we let it be. There are so many things to be excited about in education. We use technology, differentiated instruction, questioning, project based learning, guided reading, conceptual math, and higher level thinking skills to meet student needs and support them as individual learners. We are part of a journey to teach 21st Century skills to students who may find the cure for cancer, save endangered species, convert our energy sources into renewable energy for a greener planet, and lead our world beyond what we even know as possible today.

As you walk through the heavy doors of our school buildings each morning or tiredly stagger through our own doors at night, stop a minute and think. Think about the possibility around you. Think about how to surround yourself with positive people. Think about ways to surround yourself with support. Think about connecting online through social media that supports education. Read and think about articles by others who are in the field with you doing the work through free publications (hey, we are on a teacher's salary) like *The Educator's Room*. There are resources at your fingertips to stretch your teaching in technology and project based learning and differentiation and questioning. In this time of teaching, we have more resources than we can possibly use in a year. Find those that match your philosophy and content and curriculum and have fun with your students. Think about what brought you here and where you want to go.

Henry David Thoreau said, "As a single footstep will not make a path on the earth, so a single thought will not make a pathway in the mind. To make a deep physical path, we walk again and again. To make a deep mental path, we must think over and over the kind of thoughts we wish to dominate our lives." You are here because you want to be part of this journey. Your inner teacher has led you to explore and find answers to keep you in the work of children. There are answers. There are possibilities. You are here for a reason. There is a place for you to go next in education.

Our educational system has been through many changes and there will be many more to come. You are part of this path, walking along, but you are not alone. You can choose to walk with your students and lead them into their futures so they become part of the path. You can choose to walk with support of others doing this work. You can choose to walk with educators who are making a positive impact. "Always bear in mind that your own resolution to succeed is more important than any one thing" (Abraham Lincoln). We are all in this together. As you would ask of your students on a project or assignment, "Now, is that the BEST you can do?" Go out and do your best. Teach!

Author Biographies

Katherine Davis began her teaching career eight years ago with Memphis City Public Schools. She taught seventh grade English for two years before moving to Atlanta, Georgia. Currently, Katherine teaches High School English for an urban school district in Atlanta, Georgia. She has taught classes ranging from remedial to AP courses. Her areas of expertise include: common core standards, curriculum, assessment, and instruction, and new teacher support.

In addition to teaching, Katherine is a Common Core State Facilitator, English/ Language Arts curriculum writer as well as a New Teacher Mentor. She has also presented at conferences on the district, state, and national level pertaining to increasing student achievement in writing.

Katherine received a bachelor's degree in English from the University of Memphis, a bachelor's degree in Education from Crichton College (Memphis, TN), and both a Master's of Education in Curriculum, Assessment, and Instruction and an Education Specialist degree in Teacher Leadership from Walden University.

Katherine is currently completing her doctorate degree and has plans of opening her own school. In her spare time, she likes to check things off of her bucket list. Skydiving was recently checked off.

Email:kamdavis11@gmail.com

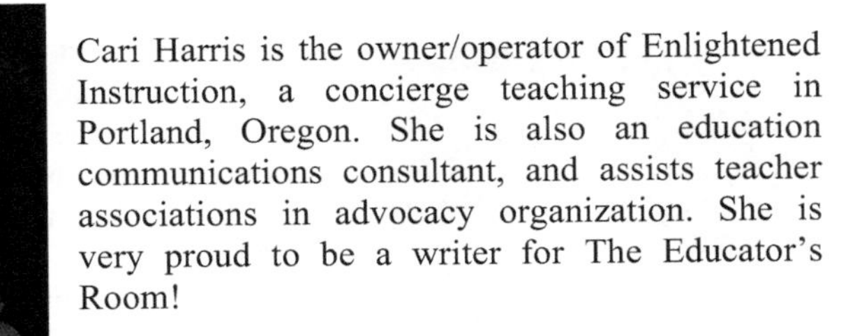

Cari Harris is the owner/operator of Enlightened Instruction, a concierge teaching service in Portland, Oregon. She is also an education communications consultant, and assists teacher associations in advocacy organization. She is very proud to be a writer for The Educator's Room!

Cari has been a high school Social Sciences teacher for over eight years and has taught every secondary level, from remedial to AP college courses in both public and private schools. She has many years of experience in high poverty, urban student populations, and has also designed curriculum and taught in small community-based student groups. Her areas of expertise are Conflict Management, Civic Education and Participation, and Social Justice Curriculum at a secondary and college level.

Prior to her teaching career, Cari worked for 15 years in the legal world, and was a human rights activist in Northern Ireland and Washington, DC. She earned her bachelor's in Conflict Analysis & Resolution from George Mason University, her Master's in Teaching from Lewis & Clark Graduate School, and is currently completing a Masters in Political Science from Virginia Tech University. In 2009, she was chosen as a James Madison Fellow, a Congressional Fellowship designed for teachers of Constitution-based social sciences. Meanwhile, she is a single mom to her ten-year-old son, and frequently loses to him when they play *Settlers of Cataan*.

You can find her on Twitter @teachacari, or online at http://EnlightenedInstruction.com.

Jania Hoover, Ed. D., is a high school teacher in Atlanta, Georgia. For the past eight years, she has taught several challenging student populations at both traditional and non-traditional schools in the Atlanta area. Her areas of expertise include standards-based grading, alternative assessment and new teacher support.

In addition to teaching a variety of high school social studies classes, Jania is a curriculum writer and teacher trainer. She has presented to educators at the school, district, and national level. Jania is one of the original writers for The Educator's Room online magazine.

Jania received her bachelor's degree from Loyola Marymount University, her Master's of Education from the University of Georgia, and her doctorate of education in School Improvement from the University of West Georgia. Her dissertation focused on the contributions of Africa-related topics to the world history curriculum and textbooks in Georgia.

Jania grew up in Honolulu, Hawaii and currently lives in Riverdale, Georgia. She once ran 26.2 miles for fun.

Twitter: @drjhoov
Email: drjhoover@gmail.com

Cindy Lumpkin, better known as The LD Coach, holds a Masters in Educational Leadership and Administration. She has taught Special Education in a large urban school district for almost 10 years. Currently she serves as Executive Director of TRIUMPH in Life, Inc., an organization she founded to empower students with learning disabilities to reach their full potential in life.

She also openly speaks about her own struggle of growing up with a learning disability and presents workshops and keynotes on areas impacting Special Education and overcoming obstacles in life. Cindy is the author of *Destined for Success and In Search of True Beauty* and contributing author of *Confidence to Greatness for Teenage Girls.* She writes regularly for BLOG Magazine and The Educator's Room.

Connect with Cindy at www.cindylumpkin.org, via Facebook at http://www.facebook.com/cindylumpkin or twitter @TheLDCoach.

Lori Heather Rice is a sixteen year survivor of the educational system as a classroom teacher, and has been nominated for and received many awards during her teaching career. She began teaching in 1996 in the very elementary school she attended as a child. She attended Kansas State University and received a duel B.S. in Elementary Education and Early Childhood Education. She lives across the river from her parents in a small rural town.

Lori has been nominated for the Presidential Award for Excellence in Science, was USD 320 Elementary Teacher of the Year in 2010, was a Region 2 semi-finalist for Kansas Teacher of the Year 2011, and has received numerous grants. Lori has taught K-2 reading, kindergarten, first grade, looping K-1, and fourth grade. Her passion is helping students think critically using effective questioning and differentiated instruction. Lori enjoys learning, reading, playing with her own children, and questioning, so the endless queries of fourth graders make her smile instead of frown. In her spare time she scrapbooks the life and events of her three children and has recently started running 5K races with a group of teacher friends.

A teacher, first and foremost, Lori also writes, blogs, and provides professional development for educators. She can be contacted at loririce@wamego.net or through her blog www.riceclassroom.com.

Sarah Sorge is a New York State certified science teacher who has taught Biology, Physical Science, Earth Science, Health, and Nanoscience/Nanotechnology at the junior high and high school level for the past several years. Her education includes a B.S. in Biology, a M.S. in Liberal Studies with a Biology/English concentration, and advanced studies in adolescent education.

She is currently acting as the science department chairperson at her school, a participant in a STEM initiative grant in her school district whose aim is to bring problem-based learning strategies and STEM techniques across all disciplines, and part-time Biology professor in a local college. Sarah's interests include neuroscience in education and teaching to the senses of her students; her future ambition is to earn her doctorate degree in educational neurobiology or cognitive neuroscience with an education concentration.

Email: ms.sarah.sorge@gmail.com
Facebook: https://www.facebook.com/sarah.sorge

Franchesca Warren is the Publisher & Owner of The Educator's Room, LLC the first online educational magazine dedicated to showing that teachers are indeed the experts in education. For the past ten years, she has taught a variety of high school classes ranging from remedial courses to AP Level courses all in Title I schools in both the Atlanta metro areas and in Memphis, TN. Her areas of expertise include: Common Core Implementation, alternative assessment and supporting new teachers in urban schools.

In addition to teaching, Franchesca has also written curriculum and presented at conferences on a variety of educational issues. In 2012, Franchesca started the first online magazine dedicated to empowering teachers as the experts in the classroom, The Educator's Room. Through this magazine, Franchesca has had a chance to work with writers across the country as they attempt to help teachers around the world, realize their expertise.

A native of Kentucky, Franchesca received both her bachelor's degree from The University of Memphis and her Master's in Instruction and Curriculum. In her spare time, she enjoys spending time with her family of five and running an occasional half marathon.

Twitter: @educatorsroom
Email: info@theeducatorsroom.com

Check out these authors and more amazing educators & writers at:

www.theeducatorsroom.com